The Mountain of Fire

by Peter Millett

illustrated by Giorgio Bacchin

CAMBRIDGE
UNIVERSITY PRESS

Institute of Education

Chapter One

Jun and her school friends, Rafi and Daniel, sat quietly in the tourist centre. They were listening to an instructor giving them safety tips about climbing Mount Merapi. Jun was very excited – she couldn't wait to climb the famous mountain.

'Listen, everybody,' said the instructor. 'Tomorrow, you are going to climb to the top of an active volcano. My job is to keep you safe. We all have to be very careful. And most important of all, this is not a race to be first to the top. This is an experience to remember forever!'

Jun smiled at Daniel. 'The rest of the class is lucky that it's not a race. No one would have a chance of beating me to the top!' she said.

Before Daniel could reply, the climbing instructor pointed at Jun. 'Remind me of our golden rule for tomorrow.'

'Ah, speed,' Jun mumbled. 'Er no, I mean *safety*,' she corrected herself. Her friends giggled.

The instructor frowned.

Early the next morning, they met Agus, their guide, at the foot of the mountain.

'Mount Merapi can be very dangerous,' he explained. 'We need to take care to stick together, otherwise you can get lost or hurt yourself. There will be no one to help you up there. And remember, this is an active volcano. There have been one or two small tremors recently. If I say we have to turn back, we do exactly that!'

'Yes, of course,' said Jun. 'But I'm going to be first to the top,' she muttered to herself.

After an hour of climbing, Jun had already pushed her way to the front of the group. Daniel and Rafi jogged after her, reluctantly.

'Remember, it's an *experience*,' Rafi cried.

'Yeah – I want to experience being first up the mountain,' laughed Jun.

'Hey, you at the front, please slow down,' Agus cried. 'I must be able to see you at all times. Climbing Mount Merapi is very risky. Your life is in my hands.'

Chapter Two

Jun, Daniel and Rafi ignored Agus. They separated from the group. Soon, they were far ahead of their classmates.

Agus came charging up towards them.

'You **must** do as I say,' he said, sternly. 'This journey can be really dangerous.'

Daniel glared at Jun.

'I'm sorry,' said Jun. 'But everyone else is moving so slowly today. I can't hold back my excitement about climbing to the top.'

'I told you yesterday, this is not a race,' Agus snapped.

Just then, the ground rumbled and shuddered.

'What was that?' cried Rafi.

Agus grabbed his radio phone. 'Abandon summit climb,' he shouted. 'Return to base.'

'What?' Daniel said.

Agus turned to the three friends. 'We're going back right now. We have to leave immediately.'

'We have to leave now?' Rafi cried. 'But … but we've only just got here.'

Suddenly, the ground shook violently. Agus and the group almost fell to the ground.

'Emergency!' Agus shouted into his phone. 'Repeat, emergency!'

Then *boom*, a huge explosion sent lava flying up into the morning sky.

'Everybody, run for your lives!' Agus shouted.

Jun, Rafi and Daniel tossed their bags to the ground and sprinted after Agus.

'Hurry! Follow me!' he yelled. 'The reports said the mountain was safe today but they were *wrong!*'

Two car-sized boulders fell from the sky. Another smashed into the mountainside immediately behind them.

The group followed Agus. They skidded on their backs down a long slope.

'Are we going to die?' Rafi cried.

No one answered as a deafening roar thundered across the mountain top.

9

Chapter Three

The sky turned dark.
Lightning bolts lit up the top
of the mountain.

Daniel ran as fast as he could.
'I'm really scared,' he panted.

'Just keep running,' Rafi shouted.
'See if you can outrun me.'

Agus pointed to his left.
'This way,' he said. 'If we can find
some cover, we might survive
the initial blast.'

Daniel, Rafi and Jun ran
closely behind Agus and darted
into a thick forest.

'Cover your faces,' Agus said.
'Don't breathe in the smoke.'

Jun helped Rafi cover his face.

They hurtled through the forest undergrowth. Ahead of them in the distance, they saw some of the slower runners from the main group.

Daniel stepped to his left to avoid a steep bank, but he hadn't seen the pothole. He twisted his ankle sharply and fell to his knees in agony.

Agus stopped to help him. Daniel was clutching at his foot with tears in his eyes.

'Go ... go ... go!' Agus yelled. 'You need to keep on running.'

But Jun stood her ground. 'You go, Rafi,' she said. 'It's my fault we're so far behind the others. I'll stay back with Daniel.'

Rafi turned and watched the last members of the other group disappear out of sight.

'Quick – you might still be able to catch them,' said Jun.

Rafi took a deep breath and reluctantly headed off down the winding path. Broken trees and smouldering ash fell around him.

'See you at the bottom,' Jun cried out.

'Hopefully ...' Rafi shouted back over his shoulder.

Agus slid Daniel on his back and lifted him up off the ground. 'Okay, let's keep going,' he said, gritting his teeth.

'LOOK!' Daniel shouted. He pointed to a burning, orange trail scorching across the ground, one hundred metres to their left.

'Lava flows!' Agus groaned. 'Let's move as fast as we can to a new escape path.'

The lava spilled down into the valley. Then it swung around and changed direction towards them.

'Go right. Go right!' Agus yelled. He pushed on with Daniel riding uncomfortably on his back.

Jun ran as fast as she could through the forest undergrowth.

Above her, tree tops were aflame with the molten rain pelting down from the sky. Everywhere, ash fell like snow.

Chapter Four

They outpaced the burning lava flow, but then Agus pulled up suddenly and groaned loudly.

'Cramp!' he moaned, clutching his left calf muscle.

He gently helped Daniel down to the ground.

Daniel looked at Jun.

'I'll help you down from here,' Jun said.

Jun helped Daniel stand up and slipped her arm under his shoulder. She braced him as he began walking along, gingerly.

'We can do this,' Jun said. She had a determined look on her face. 'We are not leaving this mountain without you.'

'Thanks, Jun,' Daniel replied.

Agus limped on ahead of the others.

He got out his radio phone and started to speak.

'We're coming in late,' he said, 'but we're still in one piece. How is everybody else doing?'

Agus's face dropped. There was no reply to his call.

At last, Daniel, Jun and Agus stumbled from the forest undergrowth. They were in a clear, open space.

They looked back at the violent firework display. It seemed as if it was setting the top of the mountain on fire.

'We're safe here now,' Agus moaned. 'The flying boulders and lava can't reach us this far down.' He sat down on the ground, exhausted.

Jun helped Daniel sit down, coughing and wheezing.

'Are you sure about that?' Jun asked.

Agus nodded slowly.

'Where are the others?' Daniel asked. 'Are they okay too?'

Agus shook his head. 'I have no idea. No one is responding to my phone calls.'

Chapter Five

Suddenly, Rafi appeared. He was running up over a ridge towards them.

'You made it!' he cried. 'None of the phones could reach you. We didn't know where you were.'

'Where are all the others?' Jun asked.

'They're getting medical attention and ice-cold drinks. You'd better hurry down before they run out.'

Jun waved her friend away. 'Nah,' she said.
'I'm too exhausted to rush anywhere
at the moment. I'm just going to sit here and catch
my breath, and be thankful that I'm still alive.'

'I'm with her,' said Daniel, wiping ash
away from his forehead.

Rafi shrugged his shoulders and stared at his friend. 'I can't believe I'm hearing you say that, Jun. You wanted to be first up the mountain, and now you don't care if you're the last off it!'

'Hey, being first doesn't matter anymore,' Jun said. She ran her hands through her ash-covered hair.

'It's all about the experiences and the memories, now,' she smiled. 'We'd better get in the car. It might get hot around here.'

The Mountain of Fire — Peter Millett

Teaching notes written by Sue Bodman and Glen Franklin

Using this book

Content/theme/subject

Mount Merapi is an active volcano in Indonesia. It provides the backdrop for this exciting adventure story. Character depictions are strong to support empathy, whilst the subject matter reflects the growing maturity of the young reader.

Language structure

- The writing style is appropriate to adventure story genre, such as Agus' call on p.8: '*Emergency! Repeat Emergency!*
- Speech punctuation is used appropriately, to support reading aloud with expression and characterisation.

Book structure/visual features

- Chapters are used effectively to build tension and suspense.
- Illustrations support authorial purpose and intent, for example in depicting the characters' descent to stress the danger on p.9.

Vocabulary and comprehension

- New, unfamiliar vocabulary is not directly supported by illustrations, requiring inferential reading.
- Some examples of technical language within a fiction structure, such as '*molten*' and '*tremors*'.

Curriculum links

Science – Mount Merapi erupted most recently in 2010. Use non-fiction and internet resources to explore volcanic eruptions around the world and the impact on the surrounding communities. Why would people chose to live near active volcanoes?

Literacy – write explanation texts outlining what happens during a volcanic eruption.

Learning outcomes

Children can:

- express opinion about character and storyline, locating specific words and phrases to support their view
- recall the main episodes, ideas and events thematically rather than simple retelling
- explore personalized ways to remember the meaning and spelling of new words encountered in text.

Planning for guided reading

Lesson One How characterisation supports plot and story development

Give a copy of the book to each child. Ask them to read the title and the blurb on the back. Ask them to predict the story genre (adventure story) justifying reasons (for example, the style of the illustrations, the reference to fire). Children may have read other Cambridge Reading Adventure books by the same author ('Power Cut' at Turquoise Band, 'Sandstorm!' at Purple Band) and can compare his style.

Explain that Mount Merapi is a real, active volcano in Indonesia. Establish prior knowledge of volcano eruptions. Show pictures to demonstrate if children are not familiar with what happens. Predict what might happen in the story.

Ask the group to read the first chapter, silently. Discuss the character of Jun. Look for evidence in the text that supports their opinion – for example, on p.4: '*But I'm going to be first to the top, she muttered.*' indicating she intends to go against the advice of the instructor. Look at clues in the text to indicate how her friends relate to her actions (for example, the choice of adverb in '*Daniel and Rafi jogged reluctantly after her*' on p.5).